SOUTH AFRICA

by Kate Conley

The Child's World®

Published by The Child's World®
1980 Lookout Drive • Mankato, MN 56003-1705
800-599-READ • www.childsworld.com

Acknowledgments
The Child's World®: Mary Berendes, Publishing Director
Red Line Editorial: Editorial direction
The Design Lab: Design
Amnet: Production

Design elements: Shutterstock Images
Photographs ©: Shutterstock Images, cover (left bottom), 1
(bottom left), 5, 11, 14–15, 28; Andrew Chin/Shutterstock
Images, cover (left top), 1 (top), 16 (left); Ajay Bhaskar/
Shutterstock Images, cover (left middle), 1 (bottom right),
16 (right); Nolte Lourens/Shutterstock Images, cover (right),
30; Daniel Berehulak/Getty Images News/Thinkstock, 7;
Richard Cavalleri/Shutterstock Images, 8, 24; Dominique
de La Croix/Shutterstock Images, 9; Rudi Venter/Shutterstock
Images, 12; Debbie Aird Photography/Shutterstock Images,
20–21; Wolf Avni/Shutterstock Images, 22; Attila Jandi/
Shutterstock Images, 25; Andre van der Veen/Shutterstock
Images, 26–27

ISBN 9781634070560
LCCN 2014959744

Printed in the United States of America
Mankato, MN
July, 2015
PA02268

ABOUT THE AUTHOR
Kate Conley is the author and editor of many children's books. She lives in Minnetonka, Minnesota, with her husband and two children. When she's not writing, she spends her time reading, sewing, and playing with her kids.

ONE WORLD • COUNTRIES

TABLE OF CONTENTS

ARCTIC
OCEAN

ATLANTIC
OCEAN

PACIFIC
OCEAN

PACIFIC
OCEAN

INDIAN
OCEAN

SOUTH
AFRICA

SCALE

0   1000 Miles

0   1000 KM

SOUTHERN
OCEAN

N
W   E
S

SOUTH
AFRICA

FUN FACT • ONE WORLD • COUNTRIES

South Africa has long
sunny days. This is how
the country earned its
nickname "Sunny South
Africa."

President
Nelson R.
Mandela

SOUTH AFRICA
SUID-AFRIKA   45c

CHAPTER 1

WELCOME TO SOUTH AFRICA!

Cape Town, South Africa, has beautiful beaches for people to enjoy.

Waves splash onto the white sand beach. Surfers look for the next big wave. Children run into the sea. Beach umbrellas shade people from the bright sun. It is summer in South Africa and the beaches are busy.

Life in South Africa is not just about relaxing at the beach, though. South Africans have been working hard to make their country a good place for all people to live. They want everyone to be treated equally. This equality has not always happened. For decades, the nation lived under a system called **apartheid**. It separated people based on their skin color.

Black people and white people were separated. They had separate neighborhoods, schools, and churches. Laws stopped black people from gaining power in government and businesses. Only small groups of white people were allowed to control the country.

Apartheid was unpopular outside of South Africa. Many nations refused to trade with South Africa because of it. This hurt the country's economy. Millions of people in South Africa also wanted apartheid to end.

The push to end apartheid finally succeeded in 1994. That year, Nelson Mandela became the new leader of South Africa. Since then, South Africa has been working to make all people equal.

South Africa continues to reshape itself today. It has many natural resources. Its mines are filled with gold and diamonds. Animals, such as elephants and tigers, roam its endless land.

South Africa's people have kept their traditions throughout great change.

Mandela was the first black person ever to lead the nation.

CHAPTER 2

THE LAND

The temperature in South Africa never gets very hot or cold.

South Africa is the southernmost country in Africa. It is in the Southern Hemisphere, which means it is south of the **equator**. In the Southern Hemisphere, summer begins in December and lasts until March. Winter goes from June until September.

South Africa has many neighbors. It borders Botswana, Mozambique, Namibia, Swaziland, Zimbabwe, and Lesotho.

The border with Lesotho is unusual. South Africa completely surrounds Lesotho. No one can go into or out of Lesotho without first going through South Africa.

South Africa has a long coast. It stretches for 1,739 miles (2,799 km). The east coast is on the Indian Ocean. This coast has sandy beaches and warm water. The west coast is on the Atlantic Ocean. It has rocky shores, sand dunes, and cold water.

The Drakensberg Mountains run along the east coast. Snow covers the peaks in winter. Waterfalls splash down cliffs. Forests cover the valleys. Baboons, storks, and antelope all live in the lower slopes and valleys.

Much of South Africa has coast along ocean water.

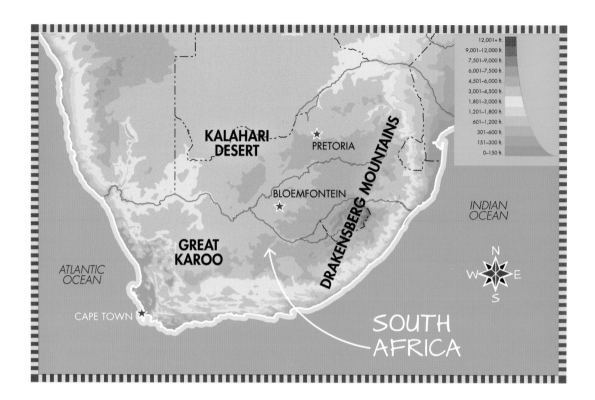

The Great Karoo is in the south. It is a high, flat area of land. It covers about 30 percent of South Africa. Most of the Great Karoo is dry, but there are some streams. Farmers grow fruit near the streams. Goats, sheep, and ostriches feed on the grasslands.

The Kalahari Desert stretches along part of South Africa's border with Namibia. The sand in this desert is red. Thorn trees and grasses grow in some parts of the desert. Most of the year it is hot and dry. Sometimes six months pass without any rain falling in the Kalahari.

South Africa has many natural resources. Its mines are famous for their large supplies of gold and diamonds. Most of the mines are near the city of Johannesburg. South Africa also has a large supply of coal. The coal is used to make electricity.

South Africa is home to a variety of wildlife. Large animals such as elephants, zebras, lions, and rhinoceroses travel across the country. More than 800 types of birds and 100 types of snakes live there, too. Most of these animals live in the country's 12 national parks. The largest of these is Kruger National Park.

The native Zulu people call the Drakensberg Mountains uKhahlamba. It means "Barrier of Spears."

FUN FACT

ONE WORLD · MANY COUNTRIES

CHAPTER 3

GOVERNMENT AND CITIES

The Palace of Justice is in Pretoria, South Africa

South Africa's official name is the Republic of South Africa. Its government is a republic. Being a republic means South

Africans vote for their leaders. The first time all South Africans were allowed to vote was in 1994. Before then, only white South Africans could vote.

South Africans choose members of parliament when they vote. The parliament makes South Africa's laws. It also selects South Africa's president from parliament. The president leads South Africa and works with other nations.

Most nations have one city that is the capital for the entire country. South Africa has three capitals. Each capital is home to a different part of the government. The president works in Pretoria. Bloemfontein is where the nation's courts are located. The parliament meets in Cape Town.

Cape Town is one of South Africa's oldest cities. European settlers created it in 1652. It was the first European town established in South Africa. Cape Town is in a bay along the Atlantic Ocean. Table Mountain rises behind the city.

Another important city is Johannesburg. It is the largest city in South Africa. More than 6 million people live there. Many large companies are located there. Johannesburg began as a mining town. Miners discovered gold there in 1886. Miners from all over the world rushed to Johannesburg.

The world of business is changing in South Africa. For many years, jobs that paid well were only available to white people. Black South Africans had fewer career choices. They also earned less money. Today, this is against the law in South Africa. Jobs are open to anyone who is qualified.

South Africans have many types of careers. Farmers raise animals and grow crops, such as corn and fruit. Factory workers produce **textiles** and food. Miners remove

After the gold rush in 1886, Johannesburg quickly grew into a large city.

coal from the land. South Africa sells its coal to countries in Asia and Europe.

The 2010 World Cup of soccer was held in Johannesburg. It was the first time the soccer tournament had ever been held in Africa. People from around the world traveled to South Africa to watch their favorite teams play.

FUN FACT • ONE WORLD • ONE COUNTRIES

South African currency

South African flag

GLOBAL CONNECTIONS

Under apartheid, South Africa became isolated from many nations. Other countries refused to work with South Africa as a way to show their disapproval of apartheid. The United States and Great Britain stopped trading with South Africa. Writers, singers, and artists refused to visit the country. The Olympic Games would not allow South African athletes to compete. Foreign businesses left South Africa.

The protests from other countries and many South Africans worked. Apartheid ended, and South Africa began trading again with the United States, Great Britain, China, and Japan. Businesses from other countries returned.

Much of the country's growing trade and business happened in Johannesburg. Now the city is called the Gateway to Africa. People and goods traveling into and out of Africa often travel through Johannesburg.

Johannesburg's O. R. Tambo International Airport is the largest airport in Africa. It moves more people and goods than any other airport on the continent. Railways and roads connect Johannesburg to other cities in Africa. This makes transporting goods easy.

Johannesburg has become an important part of many economies. Business leaders hope that the success in Johannesburg will spread to other African cities in the future.

PEOPLE AND CULTURES

South Africa is a country of great **diversity**. More than 48 million people live there. Some people are native to Africa. Others have roots in Europe, Asia, and India. South African leader Desmond Tutu has called modern South Africa "The Rainbow Nation."

Black South Africans are the largest group in the country. They make up about 80 percent of the population. They belong to a variety of ethnic groups. Each ethnic group shares a language and culture. The country's largest group is the Zulu.

White South Africans make up about 10 percent of the population. They **descend** from European settlers. The first Europeans arrived in 1652. They were Dutch. Later, settlers from Great Britain, France, and Germany came to South Africa. South Africa also has the largest Indian population outside of Asia.

The languages in South Africa are just as diverse as its people. More than 25 languages are spoken. Eleven of those are the country's official languages. Most South Africans can speak more than one language. This allows them to talk with people throughout the country.

Of South Africa's 11 official languages, nine are African. Zulu and Xhosa are the country's two most-spoken languages. Both of these languages are known for their use of clicking sounds. These sounds are made using the tongue, teeth, and back of the throat.

Other languages are important, too. English is commonly used in

About 9 million South Africans are Zulu.

20

newspapers, television, and businesses. Afrikaans is a language that developed from Dutch settlers. It mixes Dutch, African, and Indian words. It is the third most-spoken language in South Africa.

More than 80 percent of South Africans are Christian. **Missionaries** brought Christianity to the country. South Africans celebrate Christian holidays, such as Christmas. Families set up Christmas trees and give gifts. Because

Zulu people walk to a church service on Christmas.

South Africa is in the Southern Hemisphere, Christmas is in the summer. Children often spend the day at the pool or the beach.

South Africa also has national holidays. Most were created after the new government began in 1994. They celebrate the country's diversity and new freedoms. South Africans celebrate Freedom Day on April 27. It honors the 1994 election, which was held on April 27, and the end of apartheid. South African schools and businesses are closed on this day.

In 1905, the world's largest diamond was discovered in South Africa. It was called the Cullinan diamond after the owner of the mine where it was discovered. Jewelers split the diamond into nine large gems and 96 small gems.

FUN FACT

ONE WORLD · COUNTRIES

CHAPTER 5

DAILY LIFE

Many South Africans live in poverty and cannot meet basic needs.

The daily lives of South Africans vary greatly. Wealthy South Africans can afford good food, doctors, and schools. Many South Africans do not have the same options. Almost 50 percent of South Africans live in **poverty**.

Poverty makes daily life difficult for these South Africans. They often do not have enough to eat. Their homes might not

Minibuses are the most common form of transportation in South Africa.

have running water. They must use outdoor toilets and gather water from wells. Often they live far from clinics and schools.

South Africans who can afford it own cars. People walk or ride taxis, trains, and minibuses in the cities. Minibuses hold up to 15 people. They travel in and out of the cities.

Food in South Africa has great variety. One traditional dish is a stew called *potjiekos*. This dish is cooked over an open fire in a pot with three legs. The stew has meat, vegetables, and rice or potatoes. It can often be quite spicy. Another traditional dish is *pap*. *Pap* is porridge made from ground corn. *Pap* is a common dish served at barbecues. South Africans love barbecues, which they call *braai*. They grill steaks, fish, chicken, **kebabs**, and sausages. *Braai* are a chance for friends and families to gather together.

Family *braai* often take place around swimming pools when the weather is warm. Swimming is a popular activity in South Africa. Some South African homes have

Braai are popular social events throughout the country.

their own pools. The homes are usually in neighborhoods where people are wealthy.

South Africa's beaches are also popular for swimming. Most people swim at the many beaches along the Indian Ocean.

South Africans cheer for their favorite professional sports teams.

The Zulu have a special handshake. It starts as a regular handshake, the arms next move into an arm wrestling position, and then they go back to the way they started. This handshake is how you say, "Hello! How are you?"

FUN FACT · ONE WORLD · MANY COUNTRIES

The Indian Ocean's water is warm and bright blue. Palm trees, green grasses, and cliffs line the beaches.

Sports are another popular pastime in South Africa. All over the country, children play soccer. It is easy to learn and costs little to play, so children of all backgrounds can enjoy the game. Some adults play, too.

DAILY LIFE FOR CHILDREN

Nearly all South African children attend school. The school year begins in January. Most children begin school at age four or five. The first year of school is called Grade 0.

Students in public schools wear uniforms. The uniforms are different at each school. They are usually shorts or pants and a button-down shirt. Students are allowed to go barefoot at school. Shoes and socks are considered optional.

At school, students learn in the language they speak at home. In Grade 4, most classes switch to English. Many parents believe learning English helps their children later in life. They believe it will make finding a job easier.

FAST FACTS

Population: 48 million

Area: 470,693 square miles (1,219,089 sq km)

Capitals: Pretoria (administrative capital), Cape Town (legislative capital), and Bloemfontein (judicial capital)

Largest Cities: Johannesburg, Cape Town, and Ekurhuleni (East Rand)

Form of Government: Republic

Languages: Zulu, Xhosa, Afrikaans, English, Sepedi, Setswana, Sesotho, Xitsonga, siSwati, Tshivenda, and isiNdebele

Trading Partners: China, Germany, and Saudi Arabia

Major Holiday: Freedom Day

National Dish: *Braai* (barbecue)

South African children stand outside their home in their school uniforms.

GLOSSARY

apartheid (uh-PART-hite) Apartheid separated people based on their skin color. South Africa used to have an apartheid system.

descend (di-SEND) To descend is to come from a certain group of people. Some South Africans descend from Dutch settlers.

diversity (di-VUR-suh-tee) Diversity is the state of having many different people, groups, or types of things. South Africa's population has great diversity.

equator (i-KWAY-tur) The equator is an imaginary line that divides the earth equally into the Northern Hemisphere and the Southern Hemisphere. South Africa is located south of the equator.

kebabs (kuh-BOBS) Kebabs are a dish made by putting meat or vegetables on long, thin sticks and then grilling them. Kebabs are a popular food in South Africa.

missionaries (MISH-uh-ner-ees) Missionaries are people who travel to other countries to spread a religion. Missionaries brought Christianity to South Africa.

poverty (POV-ur-tee) To be in poverty is to not have enough food, money, or clothing. Many people live in poverty in South Africa.

textiles (TEK-stiles) Textiles are fibers, yarns, or cloths. South Africans make textiles.

TO LEARN MORE

BOOKS

Brown, Laaren and Lenny Hort. *Nelson Mandela.* New York: DK Publishing, 2006.

Mandela, Nelson. *Nelson Mandela's Favorite African Folktales.* New York: W.W. Horton, 2004.

Sonneborn, Liz. *The End of Apartheid in South Africa.* New York: Chelsea House, 2010.

WEB SITES

Visit our Web site for links about South Africa: **childsworld.com/links**

Note to Parents, Teachers, and Librarians: We routinely verify our Web links to make sure they are safe and active sites. So encourage your readers to check them out!

INDEX